The Champions Code

---

5 Attribute of Winners

JOHN B WILLIAMS

Contents

CHAPTER 1

Introduction to the Champion's Code

~

Understanding the Power of the Champion's Code

In the realm of athletic and executive excellence, there exists a set of principles that separates the ordinary from the extraordinary. These principles, known as the Champion's Code, unlock the hidden potential within individuals and propel them towards unparalleled success. This subchapter aims to dissect the essence of the Champion's Code, exploring its five attributes and shedding light on their transformative power.

The Champion's Code is not merely a guidebook; it is a way of life that athletes and executives can adopt to enhance their performance and achieve greatness. The first attribute of the Champion's Code is mindset. It emphasizes the importance of adopting a growth mindset, where challenges are seen as opportunities for growth and failure is viewed as a stepping stone towards success. By cultivating a resilient and positive mindset, athletes and executives can overcome obstacles and reach their full potential.

The second attribute is discipline. Champions understand the significance of consistent effort, dedication, and self-control. Whether it is adhering to a strict training regimen or maintaining focus during high-pressure situations, discipline ensures that individuals stay on track towards their goals and maximize their performance.

The third attribute of the Champion's Code is adaptability. In a rapidly changing world, athletes and executives must be able to adapt to new circumstances and seize opportunities as they arise. By embracing change and remaining flexible in their approach, champions are able to stay ahead of the curve and thrive in any environment.

The fourth attribute is resilience. Champions understand that setbacks are a natural part of the journey towards success.

They possess the ability to bounce back from failures, learn from their mistakes, and persevere in the face of adversity. Resilience enables athletes and executives to maintain their motivation and drive even when the going gets tough.

The fifth and final attribute of the Champion's Code is leadership. Champions lead by example, inspiring and motivating those around them to excel. They possess strong communication skills, empathy, and the ability to build and nurture high-performing teams. By embodying the qualities of a leader, athletes and executives can create a positive and empowering environment that fuels success.

Understanding the power of the Champion's Code is to unlock the keys to greatness. It is a blueprint for athletic and executive excellence that transcends boundaries and empowers individuals to reach their highest potential. By embracing the five attributes of mindset, discipline, adaptability, resilience, and leadership, athletes and executives can transform their lives and leave a lasting legacy of success. So, are you ready to crack the code and become a champion in your field?

The Importance of Athletic and Executive Excellence

In today's hyper-competitive world, both athletes and executives face unique challenges that require them to constantly strive for excellence. The pursuit of athletic and executive excellence is not only crucial for personal growth and success but also for the overall betterment of society. In this subchapter, we will explore the significance of achieving excellence in both realms and how they are interconnected through the five attributes of champions.

Athletes and executives may seem like two completely different groups, but they share a common goal - to be the best in their respective fields. Both require a relentless work ethic, discipline, and a burning desire to achieve greatness. By focusing on the five attributes of champions - mindset, skillset, teamwork, leadership, and resilience - athletes and executives can unlock their true potential and rise above their competitors.

Firstly, the mindset of champions is crucial for both athletes and executives. It is the foundation upon which success is built. A positive and growth-oriented mindset allows individuals to overcome challenges, push their limits, and continuously improve. By cultivating a champion's mindset, athletes and executives can develop the mental fortitude necessary to navigate the ups and downs of their respective journeys.

Secondly, the skillset of champions plays a pivotal role in athletic and executive excellence. Athletes must hone their physical abilities and continually strive to improve their technique, while executives must develop a wide range of skills such as strategic thinking, decision-making, and effective communication. By constantly honing their skills, athletes and executives can stay ahead of the competition and achieve extraordinary results.

Teamwork and leadership are two attributes that bridge the gap between athletes and executives. Both groups must work collaboratively towards a common goal, whether it be winning a championship or driving a company towards success.

Effective teamwork and inspirational leadership are essential for building a strong foundation and fostering a culture of excellence.

Lastly, resilience is a trait that athletes and executives must possess to overcome setbacks and challenges. Both realms are fraught with obstacles and failures, but it is through resilience that individuals can bounce back stronger than ever. Resilience allows athletes to turn defeat into motivation and executives to learn from their mistakes and adapt to changing circumstances.

In conclusion, athletic and executive excellence are intrinsically linked through the five attributes of champions. By embracing a champion's mindset, honing their skillset, fostering teamwork and leadership, and cultivating resilience, athletes and executives can unlock their full potential and achieve greatness. The pursuit of excellence in both realms not only leads to personal success but also contributes to the betterment of society as a whole. So, whether you are an athlete or an executive, the path to greatness lies in cracking the five attributes of champions.

How the 5 Attributes of Champions Can Transform Your Performance

In today's highly competitive world, both athletes and executives strive for excellence in their respective fields. They constantly seek ways to improve their performance, achieve their goals, and stand out from the rest. The Champion's Code: Cracking the 5 Attributes for Athletic and Executive Excellence is a book that provides valuable insights into the key attributes that separate champions from the rest. This subchapter, "How the 5 Attributes of Champions Can Transform Your Performance," explores how these attributes can revolutionize your approach to success.

The 5 Attributes of Champions are Discipline, Focus, Resilience, Adaptability, and Teamwork. These attributes are not just limited to sports; they are equally applicable to the corporate world.

When harnessed effectively, they have the power to transform your performance and elevate you to the top of your game.

Discipline is the foundation of success. By developing discipline, athletes and executives can cultivate a strong work ethic, consistency, and the ability to follow through on commitments. It enables them to stay focused on their goals and maintain a structured approach to their work.

Focus is crucial for attaining peak performance. In a world filled with distractions, the ability to concentrate on the task at hand is a valuable skill. Champions possess the ability to block out external noise and maintain unwavering focus on their objectives, leading to superior performance.

Resilience is what separates the champions from the rest during challenging times. It is the ability to bounce back from setbacks, overcome obstacles, and persevere despite adversity. Athletes and executives who possess resilience are better equipped to handle setbacks, learn from them, and come back stronger.

Adaptability is a vital attribute in today's rapidly changing world. Champions understand the importance of being flexible, embracing change, and constantly evolving to stay ahead. This attribute enables athletes and executives to thrive in dynamic environments and seize opportunities that others may miss.

Teamwork is the final attribute that champions embrace. Both athletes and executives understand that success is rarely achieved alone. Collaboration, effective communication, and the ability to work well with others are essential for achieving collective goals.

In the subchapter "How the 5 Attributes of Champions Can Transform Your Performance," athletes and executives will gain valuable insights into how these attributes can be applied in their respective fields. By embracing discipline, focus, resilience, adaptability, and teamwork, individuals can unlock their full potential and achieve excellence in their chosen endeavors. The Champion's Code provides a roadmap for success, guiding readers on their journey towards becoming champions in both their personal and professional lives.

CHAPTER 2

Attribute 1 - Mental Toughness

≈

Developing a Strong Mindset for Success

In the pursuit of excellence, athletes and executives alike face numerous challenges and obstacles that can hinder their progress. However, those who possess a strong mindset have the ability to overcome these challenges and achieve extraordinary success. This subchapter, titled "Developing a Strong Mindset for Success," is designed to equip athletes and executives with the essential tools and techniques to cultivate a resilient mindset that will propel them towards their goals.

The 5 Attributes of Champions serve as the foundation for this chapter, emphasizing the importance of mental fortitude in achieving greatness. These attributes - discipline, focus, resilience, adaptability, and perseverance - are the key ingredients for developing a strong mindset.

Discipline is the ability to stay committed to a goal, even in the face of distractions or setbacks. Athletes and executives must learn to maintain focus amidst the chaos of competition or business environments, ensuring that they consistently make progress towards their objectives. The chapter explores various strategies to enhance discipline, such as setting clear goals, creating daily routines, and practicing self-control.

Furthermore, the subchapter delves into the concept of focus - the ability to concentrate on the task at hand. Athletes and executives must learn to eliminate distractions and prioritize their attention, thereby optimizing their performance and decision-making abilities. Techniques like mindfulness and visualization are discussed to help individuals sharpen their focus and achieve peak performance.

Resilience is another crucial attribute for success. This subchapter explores the importance of bouncing back from failures and setbacks, emphasizing the need to view them as learning opportunities rather than roadblocks. Athletes and executives are encouraged to develop a growth mindset, embrace challenges, and persevere in the face of adversity.

In an ever-changing world, adaptability is a skill that separates champions from the rest. This subchapter highlights the significance of embracing change, being open to new ideas, and developing the ability to adjust strategies and tactics as needed. Athletes and executives are provided with practical techniques to enhance their adaptability and thrive in dynamic environments.

Lastly, perseverance is explored as the attribute that keeps athletes and executives going when others might give up. This subchapter emphasizes the importance of resilience, determination, and a never-give-up attitude in the pursuit of excellence.

"Developing a Strong Mindset for Success" is a valuable resource for athletes and executives seeking to unlock their full potential. By mastering the 5 Attributes of Champions - discipline, focus, resilience, adaptability, and perseverance - individuals can cultivate a mindset that will propel them towards their goals, both in the athletic arena and the business world.

Strategies for Overcoming Mental Barriers

In the fast-paced world of sports and executive success, mental barriers can often hinder progress and prevent individuals from reaching their full potential. These barriers can manifest in various forms, such as self-doubt, fear of failure, or a lack of focus and confidence. However, with the right strategies, athletes and executives can overcome these mental barriers and unlock their true potential. This subchapter explores effective strategies for overcoming these obstacles, enabling individuals to harness the five attributes of champions.

1. Embrace a Growth Mindset:

One of the most powerful strategies for overcoming mental barriers is to adopt a growth mindset. This mindset allows athletes and executives to view challenges as opportunities for growth and learning. By reframing setbacks as valuable experiences, individuals can develop resilience and perseverance, enabling them to push through mental barriers and achieve success.

2. Visualize Success:

Visualization is a powerful tool that can help athletes and executives overcome mental barriers. By vividly imagining themselves succeeding and achieving their goals, individuals can boost their confidence and belief in their abilities. Regular visualization exercises can rewire the brain, allowing individuals to overcome self-doubt and build mental strength.

3. Develop a Strong Support System:

Surrounding oneself with a supportive and like-minded community is crucial in overcoming mental barriers. Athletes and executives should seek out mentors, coaches, or peers who can provide guidance, motivation, and constructive feedback. A strong support system can help individuals stay accountable, provide valuable insights, and offer encouragement during challenging times.

4. Practice Mindfulness and Stress Management:

In the face of mental barriers, practicing mindfulness and stress management techniques can be highly beneficial.

Mindfulness exercises, such as meditation or deep breathing, can help individuals stay present and focused, reducing anxiety and fear. Additionally, adopting stress management techniques like exercise, adequate sleep, and relaxation techniques can promote mental clarity and resilience.

5. Set Realistic Goals and Celebrate Milestones:

Setting realistic goals and celebrating milestones along the way can boost motivation and confidence, helping individuals overcome mental barriers. By breaking large goals into smaller, achievable steps, athletes and executives can maintain a sense of progress and momentum. Celebrating milestones, no matter how small, reinforces positive behaviors and provides a sense of accomplishment.

By implementing these strategies, athletes and executives can overcome mental barriers and unlock the five attributes of champions: resilience, focus, confidence, adaptability, and perseverance. With a growth mindset, visualization techniques, a strong support system, mindfulness, and goal- setting, individuals can overcome self-imposed limitations and achieve excellence in both athletic and executive pursuits.

Building Resilience and Bouncing Back from Setbacks

In the journey towards excellence, setbacks are inevitable. Whether you are an athlete striving for greatness or an executive aiming for success, the ability to bounce back from setbacks is a crucial skill that separates champions from the rest. Resilience is the key to overcoming obstacles, adapting to change, and ultimately achieving greatness.

In this subchapter, we will delve into the importance of building resilience and provide practical strategies to help athletes and executives develop this essential attribute. By understanding the five attributes of champions and how they relate to resilience, you will be equipped with the tools to face adversity head-on and emerge stronger than ever.

The first attribute of champions is mental toughness. It is the ability to stay focused, motivated, and confident in the face of challenges. Building resilience requires cultivating a strong mindset that allows you to embrace setbacks as opportunities for growth. We will explore techniques such as reframing negative experiences, setting realistic goals, and practicing positive self-talk to enhance your mental toughness.

Another attribute crucial to building resilience is perseverance. Champions never give up; they keep pushing forward even when the odds are against them. We will discuss the importance of setting short-term goals, creating a support network, and developing a growth mindset to help you persevere through setbacks and maintain your motivation.

Adaptability is also a vital attribute when it comes to resilience. The ability to adjust your strategies and embrace change is crucial in overcoming setbacks. We will explore techniques such as flexibility, open-mindedness, and seeking feedback to enhance your adaptability and ensure that setbacks become stepping stones rather than roadblocks.

The fourth attribute, discipline, plays a significant role in building resilience. It is the ability to stick to your training and development plans even when faced with setbacks. We will discuss techniques such as creating routines, prioritizing self- care, and maintaining a growth mindset to enhance your discipline and bounce back from setbacks stronger than ever.

Lastly, champions possess a high level of emotional intelligence. They understand their emotions, manage them effectively, and maintain a positive outlook even in the face of adversity. We will explore strategies such as mindfulness, self- reflection, and seeking support to enhance your emotional intelligence and build resilience.

By incorporating these strategies and understanding the relationship between the five attributes of champions and resilience, athletes and executives can develop the necessary skills to overcome setbacks and reach new heights of excellence. Remember, setbacks are not roadblocks; they are opportunities for growth and transformation. Embrace them, learn from them, and bounce back stronger than ever.

CHAPTER 3

Attribute 2 - Physical Fitness

≈

Importance of Physical Fitness for Athletes and Executives

Physical fitness is a crucial aspect of success for both athletes and executives. In the pursuit of excellence, athletes and executives alike understand the importance of maintaining a high level of physical fitness. It not only enhances their performance but also contributes to their overall well-being and success in their respective fields. In this subchapter, we will explore the significance of physical fitness for athletes and executives, and how it relates to the 5 Attributes of Champions.

Firstly, physical fitness plays a vital role in enhancing performance. Athletes rely on their physical abilities to excel in their chosen sport.

Similarly, executives need to maintain their physical fitness to handle the demands of their high-pressure roles. Regular exercise, strength training, and cardiovascular activities improve endurance, agility, and overall physical capabilities. This increased physical prowess enables athletes to outperform their opponents and executives to stay energized and focused throughout their demanding work schedules.

Moreover, physical fitness contributes to mental sharpness and cognitive abilities. Regular exercise stimulates the release of endorphins, which elevate mood and reduce stress levels.

This, in turn, enhances focus, concentration, and decision- making abilities. Athletes need to remain mentally alert during competitions, while executives must make quick and accurate decisions in their fast-paced professional environments.

Physical fitness helps both groups to maintain mental clarity and perform at their best.

Furthermore, physical fitness promotes overall well-being and resilience. Athletes and executives often face high levels of stress and pressure. Regular exercise helps to alleviate stress, prevent burnout, and improve sleep quality. It also strengthens the immune system, reducing the risk of illness and increasing resilience in the face of physical and mental challenges. By maintaining their physical fitness, athletes and executives can better manage stress and maintain a healthy work-life balance.

In relation to the 5 Attributes of Champions, physical fitness aligns with the attribute of discipline. Both athletes and executives need to cultivate discipline to commit to a regular exercise routine and make healthy lifestyle choices. It requires dedication, consistency, and the ability to push oneself beyond limits. By incorporating physical fitness into their daily lives, athletes and executives demonstrate discipline and set an example for others to follow.

Creating an Effective Workout Routine

In conclusion, physical fitness is of utmost importance for athletes and executives. It enhances performance, improves mental sharpness, promotes overall well-being, and aligns with the attribute of discipline. By prioritizing physical fitness, athletes and executives can unlock their full potential and become champions in their respective fields.

In the pursuit of athletic and executive excellence, one cannot underestimate the importance of a well-designed workout routine. Whether you are an athlete striving for peak performance or an executive aiming for success in your career, implementing an effective workout routine can significantly enhance your performance and overall well-being. This subchapter will delve into the key principles of creating a workout routine that aligns with the 5 Attributes of Champions - a framework for achieving greatness.

1. Goal Setting: Before embarking on any workout routine, it is crucial to establish clear goals. Athletes and executives alike need to identify what they want to achieve through their training. This can range from improving physical strength and endurance to boosting mental resilience and focus. By setting specific and measurable goals, individuals can tailor their workout routine accordingly.

2. Balance and Variety: A well-rounded workout routine should incorporate a balance of cardiovascular exercises, strength training, flexibility work, and rest days. This variety ensures that the body is challenged in different ways, promoting overall fitness and preventing stagnation. Athletes and executives can benefit from cross-training, which involves engaging in different forms of exercise to target different muscle groups and prevent overuse injuries.

3. Time Management: Both athletes and executives lead busy lives, often juggling multiple commitments. Therefore, optimizing time management is crucial when creating a

workout routine. Scheduling workouts at consistent times and prioritizing them as non-negotiable appointments can help maintain consistency. Additionally, incorporating efficient workouts, such as high-intensity interval training (HIIT), can maximize results within a limited timeframe.

4. Progression and Adaptability: To continually improve, it is essential to incorporate progression and adaptability into a workout routine. Gradually increasing the intensity, duration, or difficulty of exercises ensures that the body is constantly challenged and does not plateau. Additionally, being adaptable allows athletes and executives to modify their routines based on their changing needs, such as addressing weaknesses or accommodating travel schedules.

5. Recovery and Self-Care: Recovery is a vital component of any workout routine. Both athletes and executives need to prioritize adequate rest, sleep, and nutrition to optimize their body's ability to repair and regenerate. Incorporating practices like stretching, foam rolling, and mindfulness exercises can also aid in relaxation and stress reduction, enhancing overall well-being.

By following these principles of creating an effective workout routine, athletes and executives can harness the power of the 5 Attributes of Champions. This holistic approach to training not only improves physical capabilities but also enhances mental resilience, focus, and overall performance. Whether you are striving for athletic or executive excellence, a well-designed workout routine can be a game-changer in your journey toward greatness.

Nutrition and Fueling Your Body for Peak Performance

In the quest for athletic and executive excellence, one cannot underestimate the importance of proper nutrition and fueling the body for peak performance. The way we nourish ourselves directly impacts our ability to perform at the highest level and achieve our goals. In this chapter, we will explore the significance of nutrition and how it ties into the five attributes of champions: discipline, resilience, focus, teamwork, and adaptability.

Discipline is the foundation upon which success is built. It is the ability to make conscious choices that align with our goals. When it comes to nutrition, discipline means fueling our bodies with the right foods and avoiding those that hinder performance. A balanced diet rich in lean proteins, healthy fats, and carbohydrates will provide the energy needed for optimal performance.

It is essential to prioritize whole foods over processed ones to ensure we are getting the necessary nutrients and vitamins for peak performance.

Resilience is the ability to bounce back from setbacks and overcome challenges. In the context of nutrition, resilience means recognizing that occasional indulgences or deviations from our ideal diet are part of a balanced lifestyle. It's important not to beat ourselves up over small slip-ups but instead to focus on getting back on track and making healthier choices moving forward.

Focus is crucial for both athletes and executives. It allows us to concentrate on the task at hand and block out distractions. Nutrition plays a significant role in maintaining focus, as certain foods can improve cognitive function and mental clarity. Incorporating foods rich in omega-3 fatty acids, antioxidants, and vitamins can enhance brain health and aid in maintaining focus during demanding situations.

Teamwork is essential for achieving success in any field. In terms of nutrition, it means involving nutritionists, trainers, and coaches who can guide us in making informed choices. Collaborating with professionals who specialize in sports nutrition or executive wellness will ensure that our dietary needs are met, and we are maximizing our performance potential.

Adaptability is the ability to adjust and thrive in changing circumstances. This attribute is especially relevant when it comes to nutrition, as individual needs may vary based on factors such as age, gender, and activity level. Being open to experimenting with different diets or making adjustments based on evolving goals and circumstances is key to sustaining peak performance.

In conclusion, nutrition is a critical component of athletic and executive excellence. By prioritizing discipline, resilience, focus, teamwork, and adaptability in our dietary choices, we can fuel our bodies for peak performance. Whether you're an athlete looking to excel in your sport or an executive striving for success in the boardroom, understanding the role of nutrition is essential in unlocking your full potential.

CHAPTER 4

Attribute 3 - Discipline and Focus

Cultivating Discipline in Training and Work

In the pursuit of excellence, discipline is the key that unlocks the door to success. Whether you are an athlete or an executive, cultivating discipline in your training and work is vital to achieving greatness. In this subchapter, we will explore the importance of discipline and provide practical strategies for developing and maintaining it.

Discipline is the foundation upon which the five attributes of champions are built - focus, perseverance, resilience, adaptability, and integrity. Without discipline, these attributes remain elusive and unattainable.

To cultivate discipline, one must first understand its essence. Discipline is not about punishment or restriction; it is about self-control and self-mastery. It is the ability to make the right choices and take the necessary actions, even when they are difficult or inconvenient. It is about staying committed to your goals and values, regardless of the obstacles that may arise.

It is discipline that enables athletes and executives to stay focused on their goals, persevere through challenges, bounce back from setbacks, adapt to changing circumstances, and maintain their integrity in the face of temptation.

One effective strategy for developing discipline is to create a routine or schedule. By establishing a structured routine for your training and work, you eliminate the need for constant decision-making and willpower. Instead, you simply follow the plan you have set for yourself, making it easier to stay disciplined and focused.

Another strategy is to set clear and specific goals. When you have a clear vision of what you want to achieve, it becomes easier to stay disciplined and motivated. Break your goals down into smaller, manageable steps, and celebrate each milestone along the way. This will help you stay on track and maintain your discipline throughout the journey.

Additionally, it is important to surround yourself with like- minded individuals who share your commitment to discipline. Seek out mentors, coaches, or colleagues who embody the attributes of champions and can provide support and guidance on your path to excellence. Their influence and accountability will help you stay disciplined and motivated.

In conclusion, cultivating discipline in your training and work is essential for achieving athletic and executive excellence. It is the foundation upon which all other attributes of champions are built. By understanding the essence of discipline, creating a routine, setting clear goals, and surrounding yourself with like-minded individuals, you can develop and maintain the discipline necessary to reach your full potential. Remember, discipline is not a punishment, but a powerful tool that will propel you towards success.

Techniques for Maintaining Focus in High-pressure Situations

In the fast-paced and competitive worlds of sports and business, athletes and executives often find themselves in high-pressure situations that demand utmost focus and concentration. The ability to maintain focus under such circumstances not only enhances performance but also determines the difference between success and failure. In this subchapter, we will explore effective techniques for maintaining focus in these challenging situations, drawing upon the five attributes of champions.

1. Mental Preparation:

One of the fundamental techniques for maintaining focus is mental preparation. Prior to a high-pressure situation, athletes and executives should engage in visualization exercises, mentally rehearsing the scenario and their desired outcome.

This technique allows individuals to create a mental blueprint, enabling them to stay focused on their goals amid distractions and pressure.

2. Controlled Breathing:

Deep, controlled breathing is another powerful technique to maintain focus. By taking slow, deliberate breaths, athletes and executives can regulate their heart rate and calm their minds. This technique helps in reducing anxiety and enhancing concentration, enabling individuals to think clearly and make sound decisions even in high-pressure situations.

3. Task Prioritization:

When facing numerous challenges simultaneously, it is vital to prioritize tasks effectively. Athletes and executives should identify the most critical tasks and allocate their focus accordingly. By breaking down complex situations into smaller, manageable tasks, individuals can maintain focus by addressing each task systematically, preventing overwhelming thoughts from derailing their concentration.

4. Positive Self-Talk:

The power of positive self-talk cannot be underestimated in high-pressure situations. Athletes and executives should develop a repertoire of positive affirmations and motivational statements to reinforce their confidence and maintain focus. By replacing negative thoughts with positive ones, individuals can cultivate a resilient mindset and stay focused on their objectives, despite the surrounding pressure.

5. Mindfulness Practices:

Practicing mindfulness techniques, such as meditation and centering exercises, can significantly aid in maintaining focus. By grounding oneself in the present moment, individuals can detach from external distractions and enhance their concentration. Regular mindfulness practices also contribute to developing a heightened awareness of one's thoughts and emotions, allowing individuals to redirect their focus when it starts to waver.

Maintaining focus in high-pressure situations is crucial for athletes and executives aiming for excellence. By employing techniques like mental preparation, controlled breathing, task prioritization, positive self-talk, and mindfulness practices, individuals can master the art of staying focused even amidst intense pressure. The five attributes of champions - discipline, resilience, determination, adaptability, and self-belief - underpin these techniques, serving as the pillars of success in both athletic and executive domains.

Creating Effective Habits for Long-term Success

In order to achieve long-term success, whether you are an athlete or an executive, it is essential to develop effective habits that will propel you towards your goals. In this subchapter, we will delve into the five attributes of champions and how they can be applied to creating these habits.

The first attribute is discipline. Without discipline, it is nearly impossible to create and maintain effective habits. Athletes and executives alike must have the self-control to consistently practice and execute their strategies. By establishing a routine and sticking to it, you will be able to develop the discipline necessary to achieve your long-term goals.

The second attribute is perseverance. Success does not come overnight, and setbacks are inevitable. However, champions are those who continue to push forward despite obstacles. By cultivating a habit of perseverance, you will be able to overcome challenges and emerge stronger than before.

Remember, success is not linear, and setbacks are merely opportunities for growth.

The third attribute is focus. In a world filled with distractions, maintaining focus is crucial for long-term success. Whether you are an athlete preparing for a competition or an executive working towards a promotion, it is essential to eliminate distractions and prioritize your goals. By developing a habit of deep focus, you will be able to maximize your productivity and make significant strides towards your desired outcomes.

The fourth attribute is continuous learning. Champions understand that growth is a lifelong journey. By establishing a habit of continuous learning, you will be able to stay ahead of the competition and adapt to changing circumstances. Whether it is gaining new skills or staying updated on industry trends, investing in your personal and professional development is essential for long-term success.

The final attribute is resilience. Setbacks and failures are inevitable, but it is how you respond to them that determines your success. Champions bounce back from adversity and use it as fuel for future success. By cultivating a habit of resilience, you will be able to turn setbacks into opportunities and maintain a positive mindset throughout your journey.

In conclusion, creating effective habits is essential for long- term success in both athletics and the executive world. By incorporating discipline, perseverance, focus, continuous learning, and resilience into your daily routine, you will be able to overcome obstacles and achieve your goals.

Remember, champions are not born overnight. It is through consistent practice and the development of effective habits that they rise to the top.

CHAPTER 5

Attribute 4 - Goal Setting and Planning

～～

Setting SMART Goals for Athletic and Professional Achievement

In order to achieve greatness, both in the realm of athletics and in the corporate world, it is crucial to set goals that are specific, measurable, attainable, relevant, and time-bound – in other words, SMART goals. This subchapter will delve into the importance of setting these kinds of goals and how they can enhance your journey towards excellence.

Athletes and executives alike can benefit tremendously from the practice of setting SMART goals. These goals provide a clear roadmap and direction for your efforts, helping you stay focused and motivated. By setting specific goals, you define exactly what you want to achieve. This clarity enables you to break down your larger aspirations into smaller, more manageable tasks, making success seem more attainable.

Measurability is another key aspect of SMART goals. By establishing measurable targets, you can track your progress and evaluate your performance objectively. This allows you to make any necessary adjustments along the way, ensuring that you stay on track towards your ultimate objective.

While it is important to dream big, it is equally important to set attainable goals. Setting realistic goals that align with your abilities and resources ensures that you do not become overwhelmed or discouraged. By striking the right balance between ambition and feasibility, you set yourself up for success and maintain a positive mindset throughout your journey.

Relevance is another crucial factor to consider when setting goals. Your goals should align with your long-term vision and values. By setting goals that are meaningful and relevant to your overall purpose, you can maintain a sense of purpose and drive throughout your athletic or professional journey.

Finally, time-bound goals help create a sense of urgency and provide a sense of structure to your endeavors. By setting deadlines for each milestone along the way, you create a sense of accountability and push yourself to work more efficiently.

In this subchapter, you will learn how to set SMART goals that are tailored to your individual needs and circumstances. You will discover techniques to break down larger goals into smaller, more manageable tasks, and you will gain insights into monitoring your progress and making necessary adjustments to stay on track.

By mastering the art of setting SMART goals, you will unlock the potential for excellence in both your athletic and professional pursuits. This subchapter will provide you with the tools and strategies necessary to set yourself up for success and achieve the greatness you aspire to.

Creating a Strategic Plan to Reach Your Goals

In the journey towards success, whether you are an athlete or an executive, one essential aspect that cannot be overlooked is the importance of creating a strategic plan. A strategic plan serves as a roadmap that guides you towards your goals, helping you stay focused and motivated throughout the process. In this subchapter, we will explore the key steps involved in creating a strategic plan and how it ties into the 5 Attributes of Champions.

1. Define Your Goals: The first step in creating a strategic plan is to clearly define your goals. Whether it is winning a championship or achieving a specific business target, having a clear vision of what you want to achieve is vital. The 5 Attributes of Champions – discipline, determination, resilience, focus, and teamwork – should be incorporated into your goals to ensure alignment with the overall champion mindset.

2. SWOT Analysis: Conducting a SWOT (Strengths, Weaknesses, Opportunities, and Threats) analysis is a crucial component of your strategic plan. Assessing your strengths and weaknesses, as well as identifying potential opportunities and threats, will help you develop strategies that leverage your strengths while addressing any weaknesses or challenges.

3. Develop Strategies: Once you have a clear understanding of your goals and have conducted a SWOT analysis, it's time to develop strategies to achieve those goals. These strategies should be aligned with the 5 Attributes of Champions. For example, discipline might involve committing to a regular training schedule, while resilience could entail developing mental toughness to overcome setbacks.

4. Set Milestones and Deadlines: Breaking down your goals into smaller milestones and setting deadlines for each is

essential for tracking progress and staying motivated. By setting realistic and achievable milestones, you can celebrate small victories along the way and stay on track towards your ultimate goal.

5. Monitor and Adjust: Regularly monitoring your progress is crucial to ensure that your strategic plan remains effective. If necessary, be open to making adjustments to your strategies, timelines, or even goals. The ability to adapt and make changes when needed is a hallmark of champions.

By creating a strategic plan that incorporates the 5 Attributes of Champions, you are setting yourself up for success.

Remember, success is not just about reaching your goals but also about the journey and the mindset you cultivate along the way. Continuously refining and implementing your strategic plan will propel you towards athletic and executive excellence, making you a true champion in all aspects of life.

Monitoring Progress and Adjusting Your Plan as Needed

In the pursuit of excellence, both athletes and executives have a common goal - to achieve success and reach their full potential. However, success does not come easily; it requires dedication, hard work, and continuous improvement. To ensure that you stay on track and make progress towards your goals, it is essential to monitor your progress and adjust your plan as needed. This subchapter will delve into the importance of monitoring progress and provide valuable insights on how to adapt your strategy to overcome obstacles and achieve greatness.

The 5 Attributes of Champions serve as the foundation for success in both athletics and the business world. These attributes - focus, discipline, perseverance, teamwork, and integrity - are the pillars that support excellence.

To effectively monitor progress, it is crucial to align your actions with these attributes and evaluate your performance against them.

Regularly assess your goals and objectives to determine if they are still relevant and achievable. As circumstances change, so do our priorities. By reviewing and adjusting your goals accordingly, you ensure that you are always working towards what matters most.

Tracking your progress is equally important. Set measurable milestones that allow you to gauge your advancement. Keep a record of your achievements, setbacks, and lessons learned.

This provides valuable insights into your strengths and weaknesses, enabling you to make informed decisions about where and how to improve.

A key aspect of monitoring progress is seeking feedback. Surround yourself with mentors, coaches, or trusted colleagues who can provide objective input. Actively listen to their observations and suggestions, and be open to constructive criticism. This external perspective can help you identify blind spots and uncover areas for growth that you might have overlooked.

However, monitoring progress alone is not enough. The ability to adjust your plan and adapt to changing circumstances is critical. Be flexible and willing to embrace new strategies when necessary. Sometimes, the path to success requires detours or even a complete change of direction. By remaining open-minded and adaptable, you increase your chances of overcoming obstacles and achieving your goals.

In conclusion, monitoring progress and adjusting your plan as needed is a vital component of achieving athletic and executive excellence. By regularly assessing your goals, tracking your progress, seeking feedback, and adapting your strategy, you ensure that you stay on the path to success.

Remember, the 5 Attributes of Champions serve as your guiding principles throughout this journey. Stay focused, disciplined, persevere through challenges, embrace teamwork, and always uphold your integrity. These attributes, combined with a willingness to monitor and adjust, will pave the way to greatness.

CHAPTER 6

Attribute 5 - Leadership and Teamwork

The Role of Leadership in Athletics and Business

In the world of sports and business, leadership plays a pivotal role in determining success and achieving excellence. Whether you are an athlete striving to be the best in your sport or an executive aiming to lead your organization to new heights, understanding the role of leadership is crucial. This subchapter explores the significance of leadership in both athletics and business and highlights the five attributes that champions possess.

Leadership is the guiding force that inspires individuals and teams to push beyond their limits and accomplish extraordinary feats. In athletics, a strong leader can motivate their team, instill a winning mindset, and foster a culture of hard work and dedication. Similarly, in the business world, effective leaders inspire their employees, provide direction, and create a positive work environment that promotes collaboration and innovation.

The five attributes of champions - discipline, resilience, adaptability, focus, and integrity - are closely intertwined with effective leadership. A true leader exhibits discipline by setting high standards for themselves and their team, consistently working towards their goals, and leading by example. They also demonstrate resilience, bouncing back from setbacks and failures, and inspiring others to do the same.

Adaptability is another crucial attribute that leaders must possess. In both athletics and business, circumstances can change rapidly, and being able to adapt and make quick decisions is essential. A leader with adaptability can navigate challenges, seize opportunities, and keep their team on track.

Focus is another critical aspect of leadership. Leaders must maintain laser-like focus on their objectives, ensuring that everyone is aligned and working towards the same goal. They must communicate clearly and provide guidance, ensuring that no one loses sight of the bigger picture.

Integrity is the final attribute that champions and leaders possess. Leaders must be honest, ethical, and transparent in their actions, gaining the trust and respect of their team members. They should lead with integrity and hold themselves accountable for their decisions.

In conclusion, leadership plays a vital role in both athletics and business. Effective leaders possess the five attributes of champions - discipline, resilience, adaptability, focus, and integrity - which enable them to inspire and guide their teams towards excellence. By understanding the role of leadership and incorporating these attributes into their approach, athletes and executives can unlock their full potential and achieve remarkable success in their respective fields.

Developing Effective Communication and Collaboration Skills

In today's fast-paced and interconnected world, effective communication and collaboration skills have become essential for success in any field, whether you are an athlete striving for greatness or an executive leading a team. This subchapter explores the importance of developing these skills and provides practical strategies to help athletes and executives excel in their respective domains.

Communication is the cornerstone of any successful endeavor. Athletes and executives alike must be able to effectively convey their thoughts, ideas, and expectations to their teammates or employees. Clear and concise communication ensures that everyone is on the same page and working towards a common goal. It fosters trust, collaboration, and synergy within the team or organization.

To develop effective communication skills, it is crucial to actively listen and empathize with others. Athletes and executives should strive to understand different perspectives, appreciate diversity, and encourage open dialogue. By creating a culture of open communication, they can unlock the full potential of their teams and organizations.

Collaboration, on the other hand, is the ability to work together towards a shared objective. Athletes must collaborate with their teammates to create winning strategies, while executives must foster collaboration among their employees to drive innovation and achieve organizational goals.

Collaboration requires effective communication, trust, and the ability to leverage each individual's strengths and expertise.

To develop effective collaboration skills, athletes and executives should encourage teamwork, facilitate open discussions, and promote a supportive and inclusive environment. They should foster a sense of shared responsibility and create opportunities for individuals to contribute their unique talents to the collective effort. By fostering collaboration, athletes and executives can tap into the collective intelligence of their teams and achieve outstanding results.

In conclusion, developing effective communication and collaboration skills is crucial for athletes and executives who aim to excel in their respective fields. By actively listening, empathizing, and promoting open dialogue, athletes and executives can enhance their communication skills. Likewise, by encouraging teamwork, fostering collaboration, and leveraging each individual's strengths, they can develop effective collaboration skills. Ultimately, mastering these skills will enable athletes and executives to unlock their full potential, foster a culture of excellence, and achieve remarkable success in their athletic and executive endeavors.

Building and Leading High-performing Teams

In the world of sports and business, success is rarely achieved by individuals alone. It is the result of a collective effort, a team working towards a common goal. Whether you are an athlete striving for victory or an executive aiming for organizational success, building and leading high-performing teams is essential. This subchapter explores the key principles and strategies that can help athletes, executives, and anyone interested in the 5 Attributes of Champions to create and lead teams that consistently deliver excellence.

1. Shared Vision and Goals: A high-performing team starts with a clear and compelling vision. Athletes and executives must articulate their goals and ensure that every team

member understands and aligns with them. This shared vision provides a sense of purpose and direction, motivating individuals to work together towards a common objective.

2. Effective Communication: Open and honest communication is the lifeblood of any successful team. Athletes and executives must foster an environment where team members feel comfortable expressing their ideas, concerns, and feedback. Regular team meetings, one-on-one discussions, and feedback sessions are essential for building trust and resolving conflicts.

3. Diversity and Inclusion: High-performing teams are characterized by diversity in skills, experiences, and perspectives. Athletes and executives should embrace diversity and create an inclusive environment where everyone feels valued and respected. This diversity can lead to innovative ideas, robust problem-solving, and a broader understanding of the challenges at hand.

4. Roles and Responsibilities: Clearly defined roles and responsibilities are critical for team success. Athletes and executives must ensure that each team member understands their role and how it contributes to the overall team objectives. Regularly evaluating and adjusting these roles can help maximize individual strengths and optimize team performance.

5. Trust and Collaboration: Trust is the foundation of any high-performing team. Athletes and executives must create a culture of trust by leading with integrity, being transparent, and fostering collaboration. Encouraging teamwork, sharing

credit for successes, and supporting each other during failures are key elements of building trust within a team.

6. Continuous Learning and Development: High-performing teams are committed to continuous learning and improvement. Athletes and executives should encourage their team members to seek opportunities for growth, provide training and development resources, and create a culture that embraces feedback and learning from mistakes.

By implementing these principles and strategies, athletes, executives, and individuals interested in the 5 Attributes of Champions can build and lead high-performing teams that consistently achieve excellence. Whether on the field or in the boardroom, the ability to create and nurture a cohesive team is a fundamental skill for success in any endeavor.

CHAPTER 7

Integration and Application

❧

Applying the 5 Attributes of Champions in Athletic Endeavors

In the world of sports, champions are not born, they are made. They possess a unique set of traits and attributes that set them apart from the rest. These attributes are not limited to the athletic field; they can also be applied in the business world.

In this subchapter, we will explore how athletes and executives can harness the power of the 5 Attributes of Champions to achieve excellence in their respective fields.

The first attribute is discipline. Champions possess unwavering discipline, which enables them to stay committed to their goals and put in the necessary work to achieve them. Whether it's waking up early for training sessions or staying late at the office to complete a project, discipline is the key to success.

Athletes can apply this attribute by adhering to a strict training regimen, while executives can exercise discipline in managing their time and resources effectively.

The second attribute is resilience. Champions understand that setbacks and failures are part of the journey to success. They view obstacles as opportunities for growth and never give up. Athletes can apply this attribute by bouncing back from defeats and injuries, while executives can learn from their mistakes and adapt their strategies accordingly.

The third attribute is focus. Champions have the ability to block out distractions and maintain laser-like focus on their goals. They prioritize what matters most and eliminate any unnecessary noise. Athletes can apply this attribute by staying focused during competitions, while executives can concentrate on the most crucial tasks at hand.

The fourth attribute is passion. Champions have a burning passion for what they do. It fuels their drive and determination, pushing them to go above and beyond. Athletes can apply this attribute by finding joy in their sport, while executives can cultivate a passion for their work and inspire their teams.

The fifth attribute is teamwork. Champions understand the power of collaboration and know that no one achieves greatness alone. They build strong relationships, communicate effectively, and support their teammates. Athletes can apply this attribute by working seamlessly with their teammates, while executives can foster a culture of teamwork within their organizations.

By applying these 5 Attributes of Champions, athletes and executives can unlock their full potential and achieve excellence in their respective fields. Whether you are on the field or in the boardroom, discipline, resilience, focus, passion, and teamwork are the keys to success. Embrace these attributes, and become the champion you were meant to be.

Translating the Champion's Code to Executive Excellence

In the fast-paced and ever-evolving world of sports and business, there are certain attributes that separate champions from the rest. These attributes, when understood and applied, can lead to both athletic and executive excellence. In this subchapter, we will explore how these attributes can be translated to the world of executives, helping them achieve their full potential and lead their organizations to success.

The five attributes of champions - discipline, commitment, resilience, adaptability, and leadership - are equally applicable to athletes and executives. While the context may differ, the essence remains the same. By understanding and embodying these attributes, executives can unlock their true potential and excel in their roles.

Discipline, for example, is crucial for athletes in maintaining a rigorous training schedule and sticking to a healthy lifestyle.

Similarly, executives need discipline to manage their time effectively, prioritize tasks, and maintain a healthy work-life balance. By adopting disciplined habits, executives can enhance their productivity and decision-making abilities.

Commitment is another attribute that athletes and executives share. Athletes commit themselves to training, teamwork, and constant improvement. Similarly, executives must commit to their organization's goals, values, and vision. By staying committed, executives can inspire their teams and foster a culture of dedication and excellence.

Resilience is a quality that champions possess in abundance. Athletes face numerous setbacks, injuries, and defeats, but they bounce back stronger. Executives, too, face challenges, setbacks, and failures. By developing resilience, executives can navigate through tough times, learn from failures, and emerge stronger, inspiring their teams to do the same.

Adaptability is crucial for both athletes and executives in a rapidly changing world. Athletes must adapt their game plans to different opponents and changing circumstances. Similarly, executives must adapt their strategies to market trends, technological advancements, and evolving customer needs. By being adaptable, executives can lead their organizations through change and stay ahead of the competition.

Finally, leadership is the pinnacle attribute of champions, whether on the field or in the boardroom. Athletes lead by example, inspire their teammates, and make tough decisions when it matters most. Executives must lead their teams, inspire trust, and make strategic decisions that drive their organizations forward. By embodying the qualities of leadership, executives can create a positive and high-performing work culture.

In conclusion, the five attributes of champions - discipline, commitment, resilience, adaptability, and leadership - are not limited to the realm of sports. Executives can translate these attributes to their professional lives, unlocking their full potential and achieving excellence. By understanding and embodying these attributes, executives can inspire their teams, navigate through challenges, and lead their organizations to success.

Case Studies of Successful Athletes and Executives who Embody the 5 Attributes

Missing Content from the pre-release version of this text.

Mike – Javelin Thrower – 2007/08

Mike was no stranger to hard work. As a young boy, he dreamt of representing his country on the world stage. With a fierce determination burning in his heart, he pursued his passion for javelin throwing with unwavering commitment.

Despite facing financial challenges, Mike refused to let his dreams slip away. Working a full-time job to make ends meet, he dedicated every spare moment to his training regimen.

Early mornings found him at the track, pushing his body to its limits under the watchful eye of his coach. Evenings were spent refining his technique, studying footage of past competitions, and meticulously planning his next moves. The road to the Olympics was not an easy one.

Mike faced countless setbacks and obstacles along the way. There were moments of doubt, moments when the weight of his responsibilities threatened to crush his spirit. But through it all, he remained steadfast in his determination, refusing to give up on his dreams. For four long years, Mike poured his heart and soul into his training, sacrificing time with friends and family, foregoing the luxuries that others took for granted. Every decision he made, every action he took, was driven by a single-minded focus on his goal: to represent his country on the world stage and to make his mark as one of the greatest javelin throwers of all time. And then, finally, the moment arrived. The 2008 Olympics were upon him, and Mike stood on the brink of realizing his lifelong dream. As he stepped onto the field, the weight of his years of dedication settled on his shoulders like a mantle of pride.

This was his moment, his chance to shine. With a steely resolve, Mike unleashed his first throw, the javelin slicing through the air with deadly precision. Again and again, he launched himself into the fray, each throw more powerful than the last. And when the dust finally settled, when the cheers of the crowd had faded into the distance, Mike stood victorious, the new American record holder and an Olympian in his own right. But for Mike, the journey was far from over. As he stood atop the podium, the gold medal draped around his neck, he knew that his greatest victory was not in the glory of the moment, but in the countless hours of hard work and sacrifice that had brought him to this point.

And as he looked out at the sea of faces before him, he knew that he had proven, once and for all, that with enough discipline and dedication, anything was possible.

Dwight Phillips – Olympian, World Champion - 2012

Dwight Phillips, the world champion long jumper, faced a significant setback when he was unexpectedly involved in a car accident and suffered a severe achilles injury.

This injury occuring at a terrible time as he was just set to begin his pre season preparation which would ready him for the upcoming championships and ensure his coveted spot in the World rankings. This unfortunate event threatened not only his career but also his passion for the sport.

Not taking the easy option by playing the victim, making excuses or complaining about how hard it would be to claw his way back to the top. Dwight decided that he would do what ever he could to make it back. Phillips exhibited remarkable resilience in his recovery journey. With focus and determination, he underwent surgery then intense rehabilitation, pushing through the pain to resume training.

Despite the initial setback, he managed to comeback and return to competitive form. Unfortunately, shortly before he was able to actually compete, fate dealt another blow when he unexpectedly re-injured his Achilles by accidentally falling down the stairs while in his home. Momentarily crushed, Phillips once again dug deep and demonstrated his resilience by refusing to succumb to circumstance. Through sheer perseverance and grit, he navigated through the challenges of rehabilitation once more, ultimately reclaiming his position among the elite long jumpers. His story serves as a testament to the indomitable human spirit and the power of resilience in the face of adversity.

CHAPTER 8

Sustaining Excellence

~~

Strategies for Maintaining Peak Performance Over Time

In the fast-paced and competitive world of sports and business, maintaining peak performance over time is essential for success. Athletes and executives alike share the common goal of achieving excellence in their respective fields, and understanding the strategies to sustain their peak performance is crucial. This subchapter will delve into the key strategies that can help athletes and executives maintain their top form over the long haul.

1. Consistent Training and Practice: One of the fundamental strategies for maintaining peak performance is consistent training and practice. Athletes and executives should adopt a disciplined approach to their craft, dedicating regular time and effort to honing their skills. By consistently challenging themselves and pushing their limits, they can ensure continuous improvement and prevent stagnation.

2. Setting Realistic Goals: Setting realistic and achievable goals is another essential strategy for sustaining peak performance. Both athletes and executives should establish clear objectives that are challenging yet attainable. These goals act as a roadmap, providing direction and motivation to consistently strive for excellence.

3. Managing Stress and Recovery: Effective stress management and prioritizing recovery are crucial for maintaining peak performance over time. Athletes and executives should learn to identify and manage stressors that can impact their performance negatively. Implementing techniques like meditation, mindfulness, and proper sleep can help optimize performance by reducing stress and promoting mental and physical well-being.

4. Adapting to Change: The ability to adapt to changing circumstances is pivotal for long-term success. Athletes and executives must be flexible and open to new approaches, technologies, and strategies. By embracing change and continuously evolving, they can stay ahead of the competition and maintain their peak performance.

5. Seeking Support and Mentorship: Surrounding themselves with a strong support system is vital for athletes and executives to sustain their peak performance. Seeking guidance from mentors, coaches, and peers can provide valuable insights, motivation, and accountability. Collaboration and learning from others who have achieved excellence can help athletes and executives navigate challenges and maintain their competitive edge.

In conclusion, sustaining peak performance over time requires a combination of consistent training, goal setting, stress management, adaptability, and seeking support. By implementing these strategies, athletes and executives can crack the code to long-term excellence, embodying the five attributes of champions: discipline, focus, resilience, teamwork, and leadership. Whether on the field or in the boardroom, these strategies can pave the way for success and ensure that peak performance becomes a long-lasting habit rather than a fleeting achievement.

Overcoming Burnout and Maintaining Work-life Balance

In today's fast-paced and demanding world, burnout has become an all-too-common phenomenon, affecting both athletes and executives alike. The constant pressure to perform at the highest level, combined with the never-ending demands of work and personal life, can take a toll on our physical and mental well-being. However, overcoming burnout and maintaining a healthy work-life balance is crucial for long- term success and overall happiness.

In this subchapter, we will explore effective strategies and practical tips for athletes and executives to overcome burnout and find harmony between their professional and personal lives. Drawing upon the principles outlined in "The Champion's Code: Cracking the 5 Attributes for Athletic and Executive Excellence," we will delve into the five attributes of champions and how they can be applied to combat burnout and achieve work-life balance.

Firstly, we will discuss the importance of self-awareness in recognizing the early signs of burnout. By paying attention to our physical and emotional well-being, we can identify when we are pushing ourselves too hard and take proactive steps to prevent burnout. We will delve into techniques such as meditation, journaling, and seeking support from mentors or coaches, which can help athletes and executives build self- awareness and develop resilience.

Next, we will explore the attribute of discipline and how it can be harnessed to create boundaries and establish healthy routines. By setting clear work hours, prioritizing self-care activities, and learning to say no to excessive demands, athletes and executives can create a more balanced lifestyle that supports their long-term success.

The subchapter will also delve into the importance of mental toughness and how it can be cultivated to overcome challenges and setbacks. By developing a growth mindset, practicing positive self-talk, and embracing failure as a learning opportunity, athletes and executives can navigate through stressful periods without succumbing to burnout.

Furthermore, we will explore the attribute of resilience and how it can be utilized to bounce back from burnout and setbacks. By building a support network, seeking professional help when needed, and engaging in activities that bring joy and fulfillment, athletes and executives can rebuild their energy and enthusiasm for their work and personal life.

Lastly, we will discuss the attribute of passion and how it can be nurtured to reignite the fire within. By aligning our work with our values and finding purpose in what we do, athletes and executives can rediscover the passion that fuels their drive, making it easier to maintain a healthy work-life balance.

In conclusion, overcoming burnout and maintaining work-life balance is a journey that requires self-awareness, discipline, mental toughness, resilience, and passion. By incorporating the five attributes of champions outlined in "The Champion's Code: Cracking the 5 Attributes for Athletic and Executive Excellence," athletes and executives can navigate through the challenges of their respective fields while prioritizing their well-being and happiness.

Continual Growth and Learning as the Key to Sustained Excellence

CHAPTER 9

Conclusion

⮾

Recap of the 5 Attributes of Champions

In this subchapter, we will take a moment to recap the five attributes of champions that have been discussed throughout this book, "The Champion's Code: Cracking the 5 Attributes for Athletic and Executive Excellence." These attributes are not only applicable to athletes but also to executives who strive for excellence in their respective fields. Let us delve into these attributes once more, reminding ourselves of their significance and how they can help us reach our fullest potential.

1. Discipline: Champions understand the importance of discipline in achieving their goals. They possess the self-control to stay focused and committed to their training or work, even when faced with challenges or distractions. By consistently adhering to structured routines and making sacrifices, champions are able to develop the skills and mindset required for success.

2. Resilience: The journey to success is rarely smooth. Champions are well aware of this, which is why they possess a remarkable resilience. They embrace failure as an opportunity to learn and grow, and they are quick to bounce back from setbacks. Their ability to adapt and remain steadfast in the face of adversity sets them apart from others.

3. Mental toughness: Champions possess a strong and unyielding mindset. They are able to overcome self-doubt, push through pain, and maintain focus even in the most challenging situations. Their mental toughness allows them to perform at their best when it matters most, and it enables them to make critical decisions under pressure.

4. Passion: Passion is the driving force behind champions. They have a deep love and enthusiasm for what they do, which fuels their dedication and perseverance. Passion gives them the strength to endure the long hours of practice, the demanding workloads, and the sacrifices required to achieve greatness.

5. Continuous growth: Champions understand that excellence is not a destination but a journey. They are always seeking ways to improve and grow both personally and professionally. They embrace feedback, seek out new challenges, and constantly strive for higher levels of performance. Their commitment to continuous growth ensures they never become complacent and are always ready to take on new opportunities.

By embracing and embodying these five attributes, athletes and executives alike can unlock their full potential and achieve greatness. Whether you are striving for athletic excellence or aiming for executive success, the attributes of discipline, resilience, mental toughness, passion, and continuous growth are the keys to unlocking your champion's code.

Final Thoughts and Encouragement for Readers to Embrace the Champion's Code

As we come to the end of this book, "The Champion's Code: Cracking the 5 Attributes for Athletic and Executive Excellence," it is important to reflect on what we have learned and how it can be applied to our lives as athletes and executives. The journey to becoming a champion requires dedication, discipline, and a commitment to mastering the five attributes that define excellence in both fields.

First and foremost, it is crucial to understand that champions are not born; they are made. The path to success is paved with hard work, perseverance, and a relentless pursuit of greatness. This book has provided you with the tools and insights needed to unlock your full potential and take your performance to the next level.

The five attributes of champions – mental toughness, goal setting, teamwork, adaptability, and continuous learning – are the foundation upon which success is built. By embracing these attributes and incorporating them into your daily life, you will create a winning mindset that sets you apart from the competition.

Mental toughness is the ability to stay focused and perform at your best even under pressure. It is about maintaining a positive mindset, bouncing back from setbacks, and using challenges as opportunities for growth. By developing mental toughness, you will be able to overcome obstacles and achieve your goals.

Goal setting is essential for both athletes and executives. It provides you with a sense of direction and purpose, allowing you to stay motivated and focused on what truly matters. By setting clear, measurable, and attainable goals, you will be able to track your progress and make the necessary adjustments along the way.

Teamwork is another attribute that cannot be overlooked. Whether you are part of a sports team or an executive team, success is often achieved through collaboration and effective communication. By fostering a culture of teamwork, you will be able to leverage the strengths of each team member and achieve collective success.

Adaptability is the ability to adjust and thrive in an ever- changing environment. In today's fast-paced world, being adaptable is a valuable skill that will allow you to navigate challenges and seize opportunities. By embracing change and staying open-minded, you will be able to stay ahead of the curve and maintain a competitive edge.

Finally, champions never stop learning. Continuous learning is the key to personal and professional growth. By seeking new knowledge, staying curious, and being open to feedback, you will be able to constantly improve and stay at the top of your game.

In conclusion, embracing the champion's code is not a one- time event but a lifelong commitment. As athletes and executives, we must strive for excellence in all aspects of our lives. By developing mental toughness, setting clear goals, fostering teamwork, staying adaptable, and continuously learning, we can unlock our full potential and become true champions in our respective fields. So, go forth and embrace the champion's code – the world is waiting for you to achieve greatness.

APPENDIX

Resources for Further Exploration and Development

⁓

Recommended Books and Articles

In order to excel in the competitive worlds of athletics and business, it is crucial for athletes and executives to constantly seek knowledge and insights that can help them reach their full potential. This subchapter, titled "Recommended Books and Articles," is dedicated to providing a list of valuable resources for individuals who are looking to enhance their skills and understand the five attributes of champions.

1. "Mindset: The New Psychology of Success" by Carol S. Dweck: This book explores the power of mindset and how it can shape one's approach to challenges and setbacks. Dweck's research on the growth mindset versus the fixed mindset is particularly relevant for athletes and executives who need to embrace a growth mindset to continuously improve and overcome obstacles.

2. "The Power of Now: A Guide to Spiritual Enlightenment" by Eckhart Tolle: This transformative book teaches individuals how to live in the present moment, fostering mental clarity and focus. Athletes and executives can benefit from Tolle's teachings, as being fully present is essential for performing at one's best and making sound decisions.

3. "Grit: The Power of Passion and Perseverance" by Angela Duckworth: Duckworth explores the concept of grit and its significance in achieving long-term success. This book is a valuable resource for athletes and executives, as it emphasizes the importance of perseverance, resilience, and passion in the face of challenges.

4. "The 7 Habits of Highly Effective People" by Stephen R. Covey: Covey's classic self-help book offers practical advice on personal and professional effectiveness. With its focus on proactive behavior, goal setting, and effective communication, it serves as a valuable resource for athletes and executives aiming to maximize their performance and leadership skills.

5. "Emotional Intelligence: Why It Can Matter More Than IQ" by Daniel Goleman: This groundbreaking book delves into the importance of emotional intelligence (EQ) in personal and professional success. Athletes and executives can benefit from understanding and developing their EQ, as it enhances self- awareness, empathy, and effective decision-making.

Additionally, athletes and executives should consider regularly reading articles from reputable sources such as Harvard Business Review, Forbes, and Sports Illustrated. These publications often feature insightful interviews, case studies, and expert opinions on topics related to the five attributes of champions. By staying informed and continuously seeking knowledge, individuals can gain a competitive edge and unlock their true potential.

In conclusion, the subchapter "Recommended Books and Articles" provides a selection of resources tailored to athletes and executives seeking to cultivate the five attributes of champions. By reading these books and staying up to date with relevant articles, individuals can gain valuable insights, develop crucial skills, and ultimately excel in their respective fields.

Websites and Online Communities for Athletes and Executives

In today's digital era, athletes and executives have a plethora of resources at their fingertips to enhance their skills, connect with like-minded individuals, and stay ahead of the game. The online world offers a myriad of websites and communities specifically designed to cater to the needs of both athletes and executives. These platforms are not only valuable sources of information but also serve as hubs for networking, learning, and personal growth.

For athletes, websites and online communities provide a wealth of knowledge on training techniques, nutrition plans, injury prevention, and sports psychology. Platforms such as Athlete Network, AthleteBiz, and TrainHeroic offer athletes the opportunity to connect with fellow athletes, share experiences, and seek advice. These communities serve as a support system, fostering a sense of camaraderie and motivation among athletes striving for excellence. Online forums, training logs, and expert articles empower athletes to enhance their performance and achieve their goals.

Similarly, executives can benefit greatly from the online resources available to them. Websites like Harvard Business Review, Forbes, and Fast Company provide valuable insights into leadership, management, innovation, and industry trends. Executives can join online communities such as LinkedIn groups, industry-specific forums, and executive networking platforms to connect with peers, engage in discussions, and stay updated on the latest developments in their respective fields. These communities facilitate knowledge sharing, mentorship opportunities, and collaboration, enabling executives to sharpen their skills and make informed decisions.

The 5 Attributes of Champions - discipline, resilience, focus, adaptability, and teamwork - are integral to both athletes and executives. Websites and online communities focused on these attributes can provide specific tools and resources to help individuals cultivate and strengthen these qualities. From online courses on resilience and focus to webinars on teamwork and adaptability, these platforms offer targeted content to support personal and professional growth.

In conclusion, the internet has revolutionized the way athletes and executives access information, connect with others, and develop their skills. Websites and online communities tailored to the needs of athletes and executives provide a wealth of resources, networking opportunities, and support systems. By harnessing the power of these platforms, individuals can enhance their performance, stay updated on industry trends, and cultivate the attributes of champions. Embracing the digital world can be a game-changer for athletes and executives striving for excellence in their respective fields.

Training Programs and Workshops for Developing the 5 Attributes

In "The Champion's Code: The 5 Attributes of Winners," we delve into the secrets of success shared by both athletes and executives. This subchapter focuses on the training programs and workshops designed specifically to develop the 5 Attributes of Winners. Whether you are an athlete striving for greatness or an executive aiming for professional excellence, these programs will help you unlock your full potential.

The 5 Attributes of Champions are the core qualities that separate the best from the rest. They include mindset, discipline, resilience, teamwork, and adaptability. These attributes are crucial for achieving success in any field, be it sports or business. Our training programs and workshops are tailored to help you cultivate and enhance these attributes, providing you with the tools necessary to excel in your chosen domain.

Mindset is the foundation of success. Our programs will teach you how to develop a growth mindset, enabling you to embrace challenges, persist in the face of adversity, and maintain a positive attitude. Through various techniques, you will learn to reframe obstacles as opportunities and unleash your full potential.

Discipline is the bridge between goals and accomplishments. Our workshops will guide you in developing discipline through effective goal-setting strategies, time management techniques, and self-accountability practices. You will learn to prioritize tasks, stay focused, and maintain a consistent work ethic, ensuring steady progress towards your objectives.

Resilience is the ability to bounce back from setbacks stronger than before. Our training programs will equip you with resilience-building techniques, teaching you how to overcome obstacles, manage stress, and maintain mental and emotional balance. By developing resilience, you will be better prepared to handle challenges and setbacks, ultimately leading to greater success.

Teamwork is essential for both athletes and executives. Our workshops will focus on building effective communication skills, fostering collaboration, and developing trust within a team. By understanding the dynamics of successful teamwork, you will be able to leverage the collective strengths of your team, leading to enhanced performance and results.

Adaptability is the ability to adjust and thrive in a rapidly changing environment. Our programs will teach you how to embrace change, think creatively, and seize opportunities. By developing adaptability, you will be better equipped to navigate uncertainties and capitalize on emerging trends, giving you a competitive edge in your field.

Whether you are an athlete or an executive, our training programs and workshops for developing the 5 Attributes of Champions will provide you with the necessary skills and mindset to achieve excellence. By investing in your personal and professional growth, you will be one step closer to unlocking your full potential and becoming a true winner.

www.ingramcontent.com/pod-product-compliance
Lightning Source LLC
LaVergne TN
LVHW051804080426
835511LV00019B/3406